Congressional Research Service

An Overview of the Tax Provisions in the American Taxpayer Relief Act of 2012

Margot L. Crandall-Hollick
Analyst in Public Finance

January 10, 2013

Congressional Research Service

7-5700

www.crs.gov

R42894

CRS Report for Congress ————————————————————
Prepared for Members and Committees of Congress

Summary

On December 31, 2012, a variety of temporary tax provisions which were part of the "fiscal cliff" expired. Two days later, the American Taxpayer Relief Act of 2012 (ATRA; P.L. 112-240) retroactively extended, and in certain cases modified, many of these provisions. The short time period between the expiration of these provisions and the enactment on January 2 of ATRA retroactively meant that from the perspective of all but upper-income taxpayers, income taxes remained unchanged between 2012 and 2013 (i.e., the amount of income tax withheld from their paycheck and the availability of certain tax deductions, credits, and exclusions remained unchanged).

This report provides an overview of the tax provisions (Titles I-IV and Title X of P.L. 112-240) included in the "fiscal cliff deal," including

- the permanent extension and modification of the 2001 and 2003 tax cuts, often referred to collectively as the "Bush-era tax cuts";

- the temporary extension of certain tax provisions originally included as part of the American Recovery and Reinvestment Act (ARRA; P.L. 111-5), often referred to as the "2009 tax cuts";

- the permanent extension of the alternative minimum tax (AMT) patch;

- the temporary extension of a variety of other temporary expiring provisions for individuals, businesses, and energy often referred to as "tax extenders"; and

- the expansion of in-plan conversions of traditional employer-sponsored retirement accounts (like 401(k) plans) to employer-sponsored Roth accounts (like Roth 401(k) plans).

ATRA did not extend the payroll tax cut. The payroll tax cut—temporarily enacted for 2011 and 2012—reduced Social Security taxes from 6.2% to 4.2% for employees and from 12.4% to 10.4% for the self-employed on the first $110,100 of wages in 2012. In addition, P.L. 112-240 did not change another component of the fiscal cliff, namely new taxes primarily related to Medicare and enacted as part of the Affordable Care Act (ACA; P.L. 111-148, as amended), which went into effect at the beginning of 2013.

The Joint Committee on Taxation (JCT) estimates that the tax provisions of ATRA (Titles I-IV and Title X) would reduce revenues by $3.9 trillion over the 10-year budgetary window from 2013 to 2022 in comparison to the official current law baseline. (The official current law baseline was an estimate of future revenue if all temporary tax provisions had expired as originally scheduled.) Of this $3.9 trillion, $1.5 trillion (39%) is a result of permanently extending certain income tax provisions of the 2001 and 2003 tax cuts, $369.1 billion (9%) is a result of permanently extending and modifying estate tax provisions, $134.2 billion (3%) is a result of temporarily extending 2009 tax cut provisions, $1.8 trillion (46%) is a result of permanently extending the AMT patch, and $76.3 billion (2%) is a result of temporarily extending certain temporary expiring provisions and "tax extenders." In contrast, using a current policy baseline which estimates future revenues if all temporary tax provisions (excluding the payroll tax cut) had been extended, the Administration has stated that these tax provisions would *raise* revenues by $618 billion.

ATRA includes other non-tax provisions, including those related to budget sequestration, emergency unemployment benefits, and Medicare. These and other policies which are not related to tax policy are not examined in this report. For an overview of all the provisions of ATRA, see CRS Report R42884, *The "Fiscal Cliff" and the American Taxpayer Relief Act of 2012*, coordinated by Mindy R. Levit.

Contents

Overview 1

Individual Income and Estate Tax Cuts (2001, 2003, and 2009 Tax Cuts) 3

   Legislative History 3

      Income Tax Provisions Enacted in 2001 and 2003 (The Bush-Era Tax Cuts) 3

      Estate Tax Provisions of the Bush-Era Tax Cuts 4

      ARRA Tax Provisions ("2009 Tax Cuts") 5

   Changes Made by ATRA 5

   Budgetary Cost 6

AMT Patch... 16

   Legislative History 16

   Changes Made by ATRA 17

   Budgetary Cost 17

Other Expiring Provisions and "Tax Extenders" 17

   Legislative History 17

      Individual 17

      Business.. 18

      Charitable 18

      Energy 18

      Community Development 19

      Disaster Relief Provisions 19

   Changes Made by ATRA 19

   Budgetary Cost 19

In-Plan Roth Conversions... 28

   Legislative History 28

   Changes Made by ATRA 29

   Budgetary Cost 29

Tables

Table 1. An Overview of the Individual Income and Estate Tax Provisions of ATRA in
  Comparison to the Hypothetical Extension or Expiration of All of These Provisions,
  2013 7

Table 2. Approximate Tax Brackets Under ATRA in 2013 by Type of Tax Filer 15

Table 3. Temporary Tax Provisions & "Tax Extenders" Which Expired in 2011 & 2012............ 21

Contacts

Author Contact Information.. 29

Overview

On December 31, 2012, a variety of temporary tax provisions which were part of the "fiscal cliff" expired.[1] Two days later, the American Taxpayer Relief Act of 2012 (ATRA; P.L. 112-240) retroactively extended and in certain cases, modified, many of these provisions.[2] The short time period between the expiration of these provisions and the enactment on January 2 of ATRA retroactively meant that from the perspective of all but upper-income taxpayers, income taxes remained unchanged between 2012 and 2013 (i.e., the amount of income tax withheld from their paycheck and the availability of certain tax deductions, credits, and exclusions remained unchanged).

This report provides an overview of the tax provisions (Titles I-IV and Title X of P.L. 112-240) included in the "fiscal cliff deal," including

- the permanent extension and modification of the 2001 and 2003 tax cuts, often referred to collectively as the "Bush-era tax cuts";

- the temporary extension of certain tax provisions originally included as part of the American Recovery and Reinvestment Act (ARRA; P.L. 111-5), often referred to as the "2009 tax cuts";

- the permanent extension of the alternative minimum tax (AMT) patch;

- the temporary extension of a variety of other temporary expiring provisions for individuals, businesses, and energy often referred to as "tax extenders"; and

- the expansion of in-plan conversions of traditional employer-sponsored retirement accounts (like 401(k) plans) to employer-sponsored Roth accounts (like Roth 401(k) plans).

ATRA did not extend the payroll tax cut.[3] The payroll tax cut—temporarily enacted for 2011 and 2012—reduced the employee's share of Social Security taxes from 6.2% to 4.2% and from 12.4% to 10.4% for the self-employed on the first $110,100 of wages in 2012. In addition, P.L. 112-240 did not change another component of the fiscal cliff, namely new taxes primarily related to Medicare and enacted as part of the Affordable Care Act (ACA; P.L. 111-148 as amended), which went into effect in the beginning of 2013.[4]

---

[1] Other tax provisions that were part of the "fiscal cliff", including the AMT patch and certain "tax extenders" discussed later in this report, expired at the end of 2011.

[2] This legislation was passed by the Senate in the early morning of January 1, 2013, by a vote of 89-8 (http://www.senate.gov/legislative/LIS/roll_call_lists/roll_call_vote_cfm.cfm?congress=112&session=2&vote=00251), and later that evening in the House by a vote of 257-167 (http://clerk.house.gov/evs/2013/roll659.xml). The president signed this legislation and it became public law on January 2, 2013.

[3] For more information on the payroll tax cut, see CRS Report R42485, *An Overview of Tax Provisions Expiring in 2012*, by Margot L. Crandall-Hollick, CRS Report R41648, *Social Security: Temporary Payroll Tax Reduction*, by Dawn Nuschler and CRS Report R42103, *Extending the Temporary Payroll Tax Reduction: A Brief Description and Economic Analysis*, by Donald J. Marples and Molly F. Sherlock.

[4] For more information on the Affordable Care Act (ACA) taxes scheduled to go into effect in 2013, see CRS Report R41128, *Health-Related Revenue Provisions in the Patient Protection and Affordable Care Act (ACA)*, by Janemarie Mulvey, specifically the section entitled "Provisions Affecting Individuals."

The Joint Committee on Taxation (JCT) estimates that the tax provisions of the fiscal cliff deal (Titles I-IV and Title X of P.L. 112-240) would reduce revenues by $3.9 trillion over the 10-year budgetary window from 2013 to 2022 in comparison to the official current law baseline. (The official current law baseline used was an estimate of future revenue if all temporary tax provisions had expired as originally scheduled.)[5] Of this $3.9 trillion, $1.5 trillion (39%) is a result of permanently extending certain income tax provisions of the 2001 and 2003 tax cuts, $369.1 billion (9%) is a result of permanently extending and modifying estate tax provisions, $134.2 billion (3%) is a result of temporarily extending 2009 tax cut provisions, $1.8 trillion (46%) is a result of permanently extending the AMT patch, and $76.3 billion (2%) is a result of temporarily extending certain temporary expiring provisions and "tax extenders." ATRA also would raise an estimated $12.2 billion (less than 1%) over the 2013-2022 budgetary window by expanding in-plan conversions of certain employer-sponsored tax-deferred retirement plans to Roth accounts. (These revenue increases were characterized as partially offsetting the two-month delay of the sequester in 2013.)[6] In contrast, using a current policy baseline which estimates future revenues if all temporary tax provisions (excluding the payroll tax cut) had been extended, the Administration has stated that these tax provisions would *raise* revenues by $618 billion.[7]

For each group of provisions, this report provides a brief legislative history of the provisions, a summary of the changes made by ATRA, and an overview of the revenue losses associated with these provisions. A detailed summary table (**Table 1**) comparing the provisions included in ATRA to both current law in effect in 2012, and the hypothetical expiration of these changes (i.e., reversion to pre-2001 tax law) in 2013 is provided for the 2001, 2003, and 2009 tax cuts. A summary table of the tax extenders (**Table 3**) and whether they were extended by ATRA is also provided.

Prior to the enactment of ATRA, a number of other legislative vehicles attempted to address these tax issues in the 112th Congress. For an overview of these bills, see CRS Report R42485, *An Overview of Tax Provisions Expiring in 2012*, by Margot L. Crandall-Hollick and CRS Report R42622, *An Overview and Comparison of Proposals to Extend the "Bush Tax Cuts": S. 3412, S. 3413, H.R. 8*, by Margot L. Crandall-Hollick.

ATRA includes other non-tax provisions including those related to budget sequestration, emergency unemployment benefits, and Medicare provisions. These and other policies which are not related to tax policy are not examined in this report. For an overview of all the provisions of ATRA, see CRS Report R42884, *The "Fiscal Cliff" and the American Taxpayer Relief Act of 2012*, coordinated by Mindy R. Levit.

---

[5] For a discussion of budget baselines, see the Budget Baseline Projections section of CRS Report R42362, *The Federal Budget: Issues for FY2013 and Beyond*, by Mindy R. Levit.

[6] For more information on the sequester, see CRS Report R42884, *The "Fiscal Cliff" and the American Taxpayer Relief Act of 2012*, coordinated by Mindy R. Levit.

[7] http://www.whitehouse.gov/blog/2013/01/01/american-taxpayer-relief-act-reduces-deficits-737-billion.

Individual Income and Estate Tax Cuts (2001, 2003, and 2009 Tax Cuts)

Prior to enactment of ATRA, three major groups of tax provisions expired at the end of 2012 (although they were retroactively reinstated for most taxpayers). First among them was a series of income tax cuts (often referred to collectively as the "Bush-era tax cuts") that were enacted by the Economic Growth and Tax Relief Reconciliation Act of 2001 (EGTRRA; P.L. 107-16) and the Jobs and Growth Tax Relief Reconciliation Act of 2003 (JGTRRA; P.L. 108-27). In addition, several tax provisions enacted as part of the American Recovery and Reinvestment Act of 2009 (ARRA; P.L. 111-5), which expanded tax credits for low-wage work, children, and higher education, were also scheduled to end. These two groups of tax provisions were originally scheduled to expire at the end of 2010 and were both extended through the end of 2012 by the Tax Relief, Unemployment Insurance Reauthorization, and Job Creation Act of 2010 (P.L. 111-312, henceforth referred to as the 2010 Tax Act). Finally, as at the end of 2012, the estate tax was scheduled to revert to its pre-2001 levels ($1 million exemption level, top rate of 55%) from the estate tax levels in the 2010 Tax Act ($5 million exemption level, top rate of 35%).

On January 2, 2013, ATRA permanently extended the Bush-era tax cuts for most taxpayers retroactively to the beginning of 2013. For certain upper income taxpayers, certain tax provisions were modified. Specifically, the top marginal tax rate on ordinary income for taxpayers with taxable income over $400,000 ($450,000 for married joint filers) rose from 35% to 39.6%. For taxpayers with taxable income over these thresholds, the top tax rates on capital gains and dividends also rose from 15% to 20%. In addition, ATRA temporarily extended for five years the ARRA expansions of tax credits for low-wage work, children, and higher education. Finally, ATRA permanently extended nearly all of the 2010 Tax Act parameters of the estate tax, except for the top tax rate on taxable estates, which rose from 35% to 40%. The Joint Committee on Taxation (JCT) estimates the extension of all of these provisions will result in $2.0 trillion of revenue losses over a 10-year budgetary window (2013-2022).

Legislative History

The Bush-era tax cuts gradually reduced individual income and estate tax liabilities between 2002 and 2010.[8] These tax cuts were extended for 2011 and 2012 by the 2010 Tax Act.

Income Tax Provisions Enacted in 2001 and 2003 (The Bush-Era Tax Cuts)

The Bush-era tax cuts lowered income taxes in a variety of ways, including by

- reducing marginal tax rates on ordinary income;[9]

---

[8] Other laws enacted during the Bush Administration accelerated the implementation of certain provisions of EGTRRA and JGTRRA or modified provisions in these bills, including the Working Families Tax Relief Act of 2004 (WFTRA; P.L. 108-311), The Tax Increase Prevention and Reconciliation Act of 2005 (TIPRA; P.L. 109-222) and the Emergency Economic Stabilization Act of 2008 (EESA; P.L. 110-343).

[9] For more information, see CRS Report R41111, *Expiration and Extension of the Individual Income Tax Cuts First Enacted in 2001 and 2003: Background and Analysis*, by James M. Bickley. In addition, see http://www.irs.gov/pub/irs-drop/rp-11-52.pdf and
(continued...)

- reducing long-term capital gains tax rates and the tax rate on dividends;[10]

- reducing and then repealing income limitations for personal exemptions and itemized deductions (often referred to as PEP and Pease, respectively);[11]

- expanding tax credits, including the earned income tax credit (EITC), the child tax credit, the adoption tax credit, and the dependent care tax credit;[12]

- reducing the marriage penalty by expanding for married couples the standard deduction, the 15% tax bracket, and the income phase-out for the EITC;[13] and

- modifying education tax incentives, including Coverdell education saving accounts (ESAs), the student loan interest deduction, and the tax treatment of certain scholarships and fellowships. The Bush-era tax cuts also created an exclusion for employer-provided educational assistance.[14]

Prior to the enactment of P.L. 112-240, all of these income tax provisions were scheduled to revert to pre-2001 levels. See **Table 1**.

Estate Tax Provisions of the Bush-Era Tax Cuts

The Bush-era tax cuts also gradually reduced the estate tax between 2002 and 2009, with a full repeal of the estate tax in 2010.[15] The estate tax is a tax on the estate of a decedent, levied against and paid by the estate.[16] Under EGTRRA, the amount of an estate which was exempt from taxation gradually rose from $1 million per decedent in 2002 to $3.5 million per decedent in 2009, while the top tax rate under the estate tax fell from 55% to 45% over the same time period. In 2010 there was no federal estate tax.

(...continued)

http://www.taxpolicycenter.org/taxtopics/TCE_CompareRates_2012.cfm.

[10] For more information, see CRS Report RS21014, *Economic and Revenue Effects of Permanent and Temporary Capital Gains Tax Cuts*, by Jane G. Gravelle and CRS Report RS21541, *Tax Treatment of Dividends Under the 2003 Tax Cut: Fact Sheet*, by Jane G. Gravelle and CRS Report R41394, *Tax Treatment of Long-Term Capital Gains and Dividends and Related Provisions in the President's FY2011 Budget Proposal*, by Mark P. Keightley.

[11] For more information, see CRS Report R41796, *Deficit Reduction: The Economic and Tax Revenue Effects of Personal Exemption Phaseout (PEP) and Limitation on Itemized Deductions (Pease)*, by Thomas L. Hungerford.

[12] For more information, see CRS Report R41873, *The Child Tax Credit: Current Law and Legislative History*, by Margot L. Crandall-Hollick, CRS Report RL31768, *The Earned Income Tax Credit (EITC): An Overview*, by Christine Scott, CRS Report RL33633, *Tax Benefits for Families: Adoption*, by Christine Scott and CRS Report RS21466, *Dependent Care: Current Tax Benefits and Legislative Issues*, by Christine Scott and Janemarie Mulvey.

[13] CRS Report RL30419, *The Marriage Tax Penalty: An Overview of the Issues*, by Jane G. Gravelle.

[14] For more information, see CRS Report R41967, *Higher Education Tax Benefits: Brief Overview and Budgetary Effects*, by Margot L. Crandall-Hollick.

[15] For more information on the estate tax, see CRS Report 95-444, *A History of Federal Estate, Gift, and Generation-Skipping Taxes*, by John R. Luckey and CRS Report RL30600, *Estate and Gift Taxes: Economic Issues*, by Donald J. Marples and Jane G. Gravelle.

[16] The federal estate and gift taxes are unified. This means that these taxes have the same rate structure. The federal gift tax is imposed on lifetime gifts of property. For more information the relationship between the estate and gift taxes, see CRS Report 95-416, *Federal Estate, Gift, and Generation-Skipping Taxes: A Description of Current Law*, by John R. Luckey.

The 2010 Tax Act reinstated the estate tax, but raised the exemption level and lowered the tax rate in comparison to the estate tax in effect in 2009. Specifically, the exemption amount in 2011 was set at $5 million per decedent (adjusted for inflation, this amount equaled $5,120,000 per decedent in 2012) and the top tax rate was set at 35%. Prior to enactment of P.L. 112-240, the estate tax was scheduled to increase in 2013, with a $1 million per decedent exemption level and 55% top tax rate.

ARRA Tax Provisions ("2009 Tax Cuts")

The American Recovery and Reinvestment Act of 2009 (ARRA; P.L. 111-5) made modifications to two provisions of the Bush-era tax cuts and enacted two new tax provisions. Specifically, ARRA's modifications expanded the refundability of the child tax credit and further reduced the marriage penalty of the EITC. These changes were extended along with the Bush-era tax cuts by the 2010 Tax Act. In addition, ARRA increased the EITC for families with three or more children[17] and enacted a new higher education tax credit—the American Opportunity Tax Credit (AOTC)—which replaced the Hope Credit.[18] These tax law changes were also extended through the end of 2012 by the 2010 Tax Act.

Changes Made by ATRA

ATRA permanently extended the income tax provisions of the 2001 and 2003 tax cuts for most taxpayers. (For a detailed overview of how ATRA extended and modified the 2001 and 2003 tax cuts, see **Table 1**.) Specifically, ATRA permanently extended the lower tax rates on ordinary income and capital gains and dividends for taxpayers with taxable income of $400,000 or less ($450,000 for married taxpayers filing jointly).[19] For taxpayers with taxable income above these thresholds, the marginal tax rate on ordinary income tax rates increased permanently from 35% to 39.6% (effectively creating a new 39.6% bracket) and the top tax rate on capital gains and dividends permanently increased from 15% to 20%. In addition, ATRA permanently reinstated PEP and Pease for taxpayers with AGI above $250,000 ($300,000 for married taxpayers filing jointly).[20,21] For taxpayers with AGI below these thresholds, PEP and Pease were permanently repealed.

ATRA also extended a modified version of the estate tax parameters that were enacted as part of the 2010 Tax Act. Specifically, ATRA extended the $5 million per decedent exemption amount (indexed for inflation). But under ATRA, the top tax rate on estates rose from 35% to 40%. ATRA also extended the gift tax parameters of a $5 million exemption level (indexed for inflation) and a

---

[17] For more information on this change, see CRS Report RS21352, *The Earned Income Tax Credit (EITC): Changes for 2011 and 2012*, by Christine Scott.

[18] For more information on the American Opportunity Tax Credit, see CRS Report R41967, *Higher Education Tax Benefits: Brief Overview and Budgetary Effects*, by Margot L. Crandall-Hollick.

[19] These new thresholds for the 39.6% bracket will for taxable years after 2013 be adjusted for inflation occurring after 2013.

[20] These new thresholds for PEP and Pease will, for taxable years after 2013, be adjusted for inflation occurring after 2013.

[21] For information on these provisions see, CRS Report R41796, *Deficit Reduction: The Economic and Tax Revenue Effects of Personal Exemption Phaseout (PEP) and Limitation on Itemized Deductions (Pease)*, by Thomas L. Hungerford.

40% top rate. In addition, ATRA extends portability rules related to the passing of an exemption amount from a decedent to a surviving spouse.

Finally, ATRA temporarily extended the four ARRA tax provisions related to the child tax credit, the EITC and the AOTC, for five years, through the end of 2017. For details on all of these provisions, see **Table 1**.

Budgetary Cost

According to the JCT, the permanent extension or modification of income and estate tax provisions originally enacted as part of the 2001, 2003, or 2009 tax cuts is estimated to reduce revenues by $2.0 trillion over the 10-year budgetary window of 2013-2022 compared to a current law baseline. Of these revenue losses, $1.5 trillion is attributed to the permanent extension of the modified income tax provisions included in the 2001 and 2003 tax cuts, $369.1 billion is attributed to the permanent extension of the modified estate tax, and $134.2 billion is attributed to the temporary extension of the expansion of certain tax credits included in ARRA.

Table 1. An Overview of the Individual Income and Estate Tax Provisions of ATRA in Comparison to the Hypothetical Extension or Expiration of All of These Provisions, 2013

Provision	Extension of All Tax Cuts *Hypothetical changes in 2013 if all Bush-era tax cuts and ARRA provisions had been extended*	ATRA P.L. 112-240	Expiration of All Tax Cuts *Hypothetical changes in 2013 if All Bush-era tax cuts and ARRA provisions had expired*
	Income Tax Provisions (2001 and 2003 Tax Cuts)		
10% Tax Bracket	This tax bracket would apply to a portion of taxable income that was, prior to the Bush tax cuts, subject to the 15% bracket. For more detail, see **Table 2**.	Same as under "Extension of All Tax Cuts." This provision is extended permanently.	This bracket would have expired and taxable income that was previously subject to the 10% rate would have been subject to the 15% rate. For more detail, see **Table 2**.
Tax Rates in Top Tax Brackets	35% | 33% | 28% | 25% tax brackets For more detail, see **Table 2**.	For taxpayers with taxable income above $400,000 ($425,000 for head of household filers and $450,000 for married joint filers), the top tax rate rises from 35% to 39.6% For taxpayers with income below these taxable income thresholds, the top tax rates remain the same as under "Extension of All Tax Cuts." This modified provision is extended permanently.	39.6% | 36% | 31% | 28% tax brackets For more detail, see **Table 2**.
Tax Rates on Capital Gains and Dividends	The top tax rate for both long-term capital gains and qualified dividends would be 15%.	For taxpayers with taxable income above $400,000 ($425,000 for head of household filers and $450,000 for married joint filers), the top tax rate on capital gains and dividends rises from 15% to 20%. For taxpayers with income below these taxable income thresholds, the top tax rates remain the same as under "Extension of All Tax Cuts." This modified provision is extended permanently.	The top tax rate for long-term capital gains would have risen to 20% and dividends would have been taxed at ordinary income tax rates.

Provision	Extension of All Tax Cuts *Hypothetical changes in 2013 if all Bush-era tax cuts and ARRA provisions had been extended*	ATRA P.L. 112-240	Expiration of All Tax Cuts *Hypothetical changes in 2013 if All Bush-era tax cuts and ARRA provisions had expired*
Limits on Itemized Deductions (Pease)	There would be no income limitations on the overall amount of itemized deductions a taxpayer could claim (i.e., the Pease limitation would be fully repealed).	For taxpayers with Adjusted Gross Income (AGI) over $250,000 ($275,000 for head of household filers and $300,000 for married joint filers), the total amount of itemized deductions is reduced by 3% of the amount by which the taxpayer's AGI exceeds these thresholds, adjusted annually for inflation. The total amount of itemized deductions is not to be reduced by more than 80%. For taxpayers with AGI below these thresholds, the Pease limitation is repealed. This modified provision is extended permanently.	The overall limitation on itemized deductions would have been restored. For higher income taxpayers, the total amount of itemized deductions would have been reduced by 3% of the amount by which the taxpayer's AGI exceeded an applicable threshold, adjusted annually for inflation. The total amount of itemized deductions would not have been reduced by more than 80%. For 2013, the JCT estimates the applicable Pease threshold would be $177,550.
Personal Exemptions Phase-Out (PEP)	There would be no overall income restrictions on the amount of personal exemptions a taxpayer could claim (i.e., the PEP limitation would be fully repealed).	For taxpayers with AGI over $250,000 ($275,000 for head of household filers and $300,000 for married joint filers), the total amount of exemptions that can be claimed will be reduced by 2% for each increment of $2,500 by which the taxpayer's AGI exceeds these thresholds, adjusted annually for inflation. For taxpayers with AGI below these thresholds, the PEP is repealed. This modified provision is extended permanently.	The limit on personal exemptions would have been restored. For higher income taxpayers, the total amount of exemptions that could have been claimed would have been reduced by 2% for each increment of $2,500 by which the taxpayer's AGI exceeded applicable thresholds, adjusted annually for inflation. For 2013, the JCT estimates the applicable Pease threshold would be $177,550 for single filers, $221,950 for head of household filers, and $266,300 for married joint filers.

Provision	Extension of All Tax Cuts *Hypothetical changes in 2013 if all Bush-era tax cuts and ARRA provisions had been extended*	ATRA P.L. 112-240	Expiration of All Tax Cuts *Hypothetical changes in 2013 if All Bush-era tax cuts and ARRA provisions had expired*
Child Tax Credit	The child credit would be $1,000 per eligible child. The child tax credit would be partially refundable using the earned income formula which is equal to 15% of a family's earnings in excess of a refundability threshold of $10,000 (indexed for inflation annually). *ARRA Modifications. ARRA lowered the refundability threshold to $3,000 (not indexed for inflation) for 2009 and 2010. This lower threshold was extended for 2011 and 2012 by P.L. 111-312.*	Same as under "Extension of All Tax Cuts." This provision is extended permanently.	The child credit would have been $500 per eligible child. The child tax credit would have been non-refundable for most families (the earned income formula would have expired).
Adoption Tax Benefits	Eligible taxpayers would be able to claim two adoption tax benefits, although the combined level of qualified expenses would be limited to $10,000 (indexed for inflation). In 2012, this limit was $12,650. Specifically, in 2012, a taxpayer could either exclude from their income up to $12,650 of employer provided adoption assistance or claim a tax credit of up to $12,650, or a combination of both tax benefits as long as the combined level of qualified expenses did not exceed $12,650. Both the tax credit and exclusion phased out for taxpayers with incomes between $189,710 and $229,710 in 2012 (indexed for annually for inflation).	Same as under "Extension of All Tax Cuts." This provision is extended permanently.	The adoption tax credit would have been available only for special needs adoptions. The exclusion for employer provided adoption assistance would have expired. The limit for the credit would have been reduced to $6,000 (not indexed for inflation). The phase-out range for the credit would have been $75,000-$115,000 (not indexed for inflation).

Provision	Extension of All Tax Cuts *Hypothetical changes in 2013 if all Bush-era tax cuts and ARRA provisions had been extended*	ATRA P.L. 112-240	Expiration of All Tax Cuts *Hypothetical changes in 2013 if All Bush-era tax cuts and ARRA provisions had expired*
Dependent Care Tax Credit	The dependent care credit would be equal to 35% of the first $3,000 of eligible expenses for one qualifying individual ($6,000 of qualifying expenses for two or more eligible individuals). The 35% credit rate would be reduced for incomes above $15,000.	Same as under "Extension of All Tax Cuts." This provision is extended permanently.	The dependent care credit would have been equal to 30% of the first $2,400 of eligible expenses for one qualifying individual ($4,800 for two or more qualifying individuals). The 30% credit rate would have been reduced for incomes above $10,000.
Standard Deduction for Married Couples	The deduction for married couples would be 200% the deduction for singles	Same as under "Extension of All Tax Cuts." This provision is extended permanently.	The deduction for married couples would have been 167% the deduction for singles.
15% Bracket for Married Couples	The upper limit of this bracket would be equal to 200% (i.e., double) the upper limit for singles.	Same as under "Extension of All Tax Cuts." This provision is extended permanently.	The upper limit of this bracket would have been equal to 167% of the upper limit for singles.
Earned Income Tax Credit Marriage Penalty Relief	The income level at which the EITC begins to phase out for married taxpayers in comparison to unmarried taxpayers would increase. Specifically, this phaseout threshold would increase by $3,000 (indexed for inflation) in comparison to unmarried claimants under EGTRRA. *ARRA Modifications: ARRA increased the phaseout threshold for married claimants by $5,000 in comparison to unmarried claimants (this amount was indexed for inflation). This modification was extended for 2011 and 2012 by P.L. 111-312.*	Same as under "Extension of All Tax Cuts." This provision is extended permanently.	The higher phase-out level for married taxpayers would have expired and their phase-out levels would have been the same as for unmarried taxpayers.
Employer Provided Educational Assistance	Up to $5,250 of qualifying employer provided educational assistance would be excluded from income and hence not subject to taxation.	Same as under "Extension of All Tax Cuts." This provision is extended permanently.	The provision would have expired.

Provision	Extension of All Tax Cuts *Hypothetical changes in 2013 if all Bush-era tax cuts and ARRA provisions had been extended*	ATRA P.L. 112-240	Expiration of All Tax Cuts *Hypothetical changes in 2013 if All Bush-era tax cuts and ARRA provisions had expired*
Student Loan Interest Deduction	Up to $2,500 of student loan interest expenses could be deducted from gross income (as an above-the-line deduction). The amount that could be deducted would phase out for taxpayers with income between $55,000 and $70,000 ($110,000 and $140,000 for married joint filers), adjusted for inflation. In 2012, these phaseout ranges were $60,000-$75,000 ($125,000-$155,000 for married joint filers).	Same as under "Extension of All Tax Cuts." This provision is extended permanently.	The deduction could only have been claimed by eligible taxpayers for the first 60 months (5 years) of interest payments. In addition, the income phase-out levels would have been reduced to $40,000-$55,000 ($60,000-$75,000 for married joint filers), adjusted for inflation. The JCT estimates the phase-out ranges would have been $50,000-$65,000 ($75,000-$90,000 for married joint filers) in 2013.
Coverdells Education Savings Accounts (ESAs)	Coverdell ESAs would be modified in several ways, including: (1) The maximum contribution amount for a beneficiary would be $2,000 per year (2) Qualified expenses would include elementary and secondary school expenses (kindergarten through 12th grade), in addition to higher education expenses (3) The phase-out range for married taxpayers would be $190,000-$220,000, not indexed for inflation (double the phase-out range for singles) (4) Age limitations would be waived for special needs beneficiaries (5) Beneficiaries who use Coverdells could also claim education tax credits without penalty (expenses paid for with Coverdell funds cannot be used to claim credits) (6) Contributions could be made to both a 529 qualified tuition plan and Coverdell for the same beneficiary without penalty.	Same as under "Extension of All Tax Cuts." This provision is extended permanently.	These modifications would have expired, hence: (1) The maximum contribution amount for a beneficiary would have been $500 per year (2) Qualified expenses would have been limited to higher education expenses (3) The phase-out range for married taxpayers would have been $150,000-$160,000, not indexed for inflation (4) Contributions could have been made up until the beneficiary was 18 years old and all distributions would have been required to be made when the beneficiary turned 30 for both non-special needs and special needs beneficiaries (5) If taxpayers claimed education tax credits when they take a Coverdell distribution, their distribution would have been subject to taxation (6) Contributions made to a Coverdell for a beneficiary would have been subject to a 6% excise tax if contributions for the same beneficiary were made to a 529 plan in the same year.

Provision	Extension of All Tax Cuts *Hypothetical changes in 2013 if all Bush-era tax cuts and ARRA provisions had been extended*	ATRA P.L. 112-240	Expiration of All Tax Cuts *Hypothetical changes in 2013 if All Bush-era tax cuts and ARRA provisions had expired*
Tax Treatment of National Health Service Corps Scholarships and F. Edward Hébert Armed Forces Health Professions Scholarship and Financial Assistance Programs	Students must generally pay taxes on any part of a scholarship, fellowship, or tuition reduction that can be attributed to teaching, research, or other services that have been performed, are being performed, or will be performed. An exception to this general rule would be allowed for funding received from the National Health Service Corps Scholarship Program and the F. Edward Hébert Armed Forces Health Professions Scholarship and Financial Assistance Program.	Same as under "Extension of All Tax Cuts." This provision is extended permanently.	Funding received from the National Health Service Corps Scholarship Program and the F. Edward Hébert Armed Forces Health Professions Scholarship and Financial Assistance Program will be included as part of income and hence subject to taxation.
Estate Tax Provisions			
Estate Tax Exemption Level and Top Rate	Under EGTRRA the estate tax gradually phased out such that in 2009, the top exemption amount was $3.5 million per decedent with a 45% tax rate and there was no estate tax in 2010. Per legislative changes made by P.L. 111-312 for 2011 and 2012, the exemption amount was equal to $5 million per decedent indexed for inflation and the top tax rate was 35%.	The exemption amount will equal $5 million per decedent indexed for inflation and the top tax rate will rise from 35% to 40%. This modified provision is extended permanently.	The top exemption amount would fall to $1 million per decedent (not indexed for inflation) and the top tax rate would rise to 55%.

Provision	Extension of All Tax Cuts *Hypothetical changes in 2013 if all Bush-era tax cuts and ARRA provisions had been extended*	ATRA P.L. 112-240	Expiration of All Tax Cuts *Hypothetical changes in 2013 if All Bush-era tax cuts and ARRA provisions had expired*
	ARRA Tax Provisions (2009 Tax Cuts)		
Refundable Portion of the Child Tax Credit	The earnings level at which taxpayers could receive the refundable portion of the child tax credit would be $3,000. *EGTRRA made the child tax credit partially refundable for taxpayers with earnings over $10,000 (adjusted for inflation). This $10,000 earnings level is referred to as the "refundability threshold."* *ARRA lowered the refundability threshold to $3,000 (not indexed for inflation) for 2009 and 2010. This lower threshold was extended for 2011 and 2012 by P.L. 111-312.*	Same as under "Extension of All Tax Cuts." This provision is extended for five years and hence expires on December 31, 2017.	The refundable child tax credit would be unavailable to most families *If the ARRA changes to the refundable portion of the child tax credit expired, but the EGTRRA changes remained in place, the refundable portion of the child tax credit would be available to taxpayers with earnings over $10,000 (indexed for inflation).*
EITC Marriage Penalty Relief	The income level at which the EITC would begin to phase out for married couples (the "phaseout threshold") would be $5,000 greater (indexed for inflation) than the income level at which the EITC phased out for unmarried taxpayers. *EGTRRA increased the phaseout threshold for married couples by $3,000 (this amount is indexed for inflation) in comparison to unmarried claimants.* *ARRA increased the phaseout threshold for married claimants by $5,000 in comparison to unmarried claimants (this amount was indexed for inflation). This modification was extended for 2011 and 2012 by P.L. 111-312.*	Same as under "Extension of All Tax Cuts." This provision is extended for five years and hence expires on December 31, 2017.	The higher phase-out threshold for married taxpayers would expire and their phase-out levels would be the same as for unmarried taxpayers. *If the ARRA changes to the EITC phaseout level for married claimants expired, but the EGTRRA changes remained in place, the phaseout threshold for married taxpayers would be $3,000 higher than the phaseout threshold for unmarried taxpayers (this amount is indexed for inflation).*

Provision	Extension of All Tax Cuts *Hypothetical changes in 2013 if all Bush-era tax cuts and ARRA provisions had been extended*	ATRA P.L. 112-240	Expiration of All Tax Cuts *Hypothetical changes in 2013 if All Bush-era tax cuts and ARRA provisions had expired*
EITC Expansion for Large Families	The EITC for families with three or more children would be equal to 45% of earnings as a result of ARRA modifications.	Same as under "Extension of All Tax Cuts." This provision is extended for five years and hence expires on December 31, 2017.	The 45% EITC for families with three or more children would expire. Families with three or more children would be eligible for the 40% EITC (which is for families with two or more children).
The American Opportunity Tax Credit	The AOTC would be in effect. ARRA temporarily replaced the permanent Hope Credit for higher education expenses with the larger and partially refundable American Opportunity Tax Credit (AOTC), and P.L. 111-312 extended this credit for 2011 and 2012.	Same as under "Extension of All Tax Cuts." This provision is extended for five years and hence expires on December 31, 2017.	The AOTC would expire. Taxpayers may be eligible for the Hope Credit.

Sources: P.L. 112-240, The Joint Committee on Taxation. JCS-2-12, The Joint Committee on Taxation. JCX-63-12 and JCX-1-13 and Table 1 in CRS Report R42485, *An Overview of Tax Provisions Expiring in 2012*, by Margot L. Crandall-Hollick.

Notes: EGTRRA refers to the Economic Growth and Tax Relief Reconciliation Act of 2001 (P.L. 107-16) and JGTRRA refers to the Jobs Growth Tax Relief Reconciliation Act of 2003 (P.L. 108-27).

Table 2. Approximate Tax Brackets Under ATRA in 2013 by Type of Tax Filer

Hypothetical Extension of All Bush-Era Tax Cuts		ATRA P.L. 112-240		Hypothetical Expiration of All Bush-Era Tax Cuts	
Single Filers					
Taxable Income (over-but not over)	**Rate**	**Taxable Income** (over-but not over)	**Rate**	**Taxable Income** (over-but not over)	**Rate**
$0-$8,900	10%	$0-$8,900	10%	$0-$36,150	15%
$8,900-$36,150	15%	$8,900-$36,150	15%		
$36,150-$87,550	25%	$36,150-$87,550	25%	$36,150-$87,550	28%
$87,550-$182,600	28%	$87,550-$182,600	28%	$87,550-$182,600	31%
$182,600-$397,000	33%	$182,600-$397,000	33%	$182,600-$397,000	36%
$397,000-	35%	$397,000-$400,000	35%	$397,000	39.6%
		$400,000-	39.6%		
Head of Household Filers					
Taxable Income (over-but not over)	**Rate**	**Taxable Income** (over-but not over)	**Rate**	**Taxable Income** (over-but not over)	**Rate**
$0-$12,700	10%	$0-$12,700	10%	$0-$48,400	15%
$12,700-$48,400	15%	$12,700-$48,400	15%		
$48,400-$125,000	25%	$48,400-$125,000	25%	$48,400-$125,000	28%
$125,000-$202,450	28%	$125,000-$202,450	28%	$125,000-$202,450	31%
$202,450-$397,000	33%	$202,450-$397,000	33%	$202,450-$397,000	36%
$397,000-	35%	$397,000-$425,000	35%	$397,000	39.6%
		$425,000-	39.6%		
Married Joint Filers					
Taxable Income (over-but not over)	**Rate**	**Taxable Income** (over-but not over)	**Rate**	**Taxable Income** (over-but not over)	**Rate**
$0-$17,800	10%	$0-$17,800	10%	$0-$60,350[a]	15%
$17,800-$72,300[a]	15%	$17,800-$72,300[a]	15%		
$72,300-$145,900	25%	$72,300-$145,900	25%	$60,350-$145,900	28%
$145,900-$222,300	28%	$145,900-$222,300	28%	$145,900-$222,300	31%
$222,300-$397,000	33%	$222,300-$397,000	33%	$222,300-$397,000	36%
$397,000-	35%	$397,000-$450,000	35%	$397,000	39.6%
		$450,000-	39.6%		

Source: Joint Committee on Taxation, *Description of Revenue Provisions Contained In The President's Fiscal Year 2013 Budget Proposal*, June 18, 2012, JCS-2-12, Tables 5 & 6 and P.L. 112-240, the American Taxpayer Relief Act of 2012.

Notes: These brackets are based on estimates of the individual income rate structure in 2013 from the Joint Committee on Taxation and the statutory levels for the 39.6% bracket as included in P.L. 112-240. Aside from the 39.6% bracket, the actual brackets for 2013 may differ.

a. For married joint filers, if the Bush-era tax cuts had expired, the top of the 15% bracket would have been equal to 167% of the top of the 15% bracket for singles. The extension of the Bush-era tax cuts extended the provision whereby the 15% bracket for married joint filers is 200% the bracket for singles.

AMT Patch

Legislative History

The Alternative Minimum Tax (AMT) was designed to ensure that higher-income taxpayers who owed little or no taxes under the regular income tax because they could claim tax preferences would still pay some tax.[22] When calculating the AMT, taxpayers first add back various "tax preference items" (like certain deductions) to their taxable income to determine the amount of income subject to the AMT (the "AMT tax base"). Second, taxpayers subtract a basic exemption amount from their AMT tax base. Third, a two-tiered rate structure of 26% and 28% is assessed against the AMT tax base to determine tax liability. Finally, if a taxpayer's AMT is greater than their regular tax liability, the taxpayer pays the difference in addition to their regular tax liability. Crucially, prior to the enactment of P.L. 112-240, key parts of the AMT—including the exemption amount—were not indexed for inflation. This meant that an additional 28 million taxpayers would have been subject to the AMT in 2012 due to the rise of their nominal income levels over time.[23]

The Bush-era tax cuts temporarily increased the exemption amount under the AMT. This temporary increase in the exemption amount, known as the AMT patch, was extended several more times[24] and was in effect through the end of 2011.[25] Prior to enactment of ATRA, the AMT patch had expired for 2012. In 2011, the AMT exemption amounts were $74,450 for married individuals filing joint returns and $48,450 for unmarried individuals. Before enactment of ATRA, these exemption amounts would have reverted to $45,000 for married individuals and $33,750 for unmarried individuals beginning in 2012.[26] In addition, past AMT patch legislation has included a provision allowing taxpayers to reduce their AMT by nonrefundable personal tax credits.[27] Without a patch, most nonrefundable personal credits would have no longer been allowed against the AMT.

---

[22] For more information on the Alternative Minimum Tax, see CRS Report RL30149, *The Alternative Minimum Tax for Individuals*, by Steven Maguire.

[23] Tax Policy Center, Table T12-0168, http://www.taxpolicycenter.org/numbers/displayatab.cfm?Docid=3511& DocTypeID=7.

[24] For more information, see http://www.taxpolicycenter.org/taxfacts/displayafact.cfm?Docid=195. In addition, see CRS Report RL30149, *The Alternative Minimum Tax for Individuals*, by Steven Maguire.

[25] The last AMT patch which was included in P.L. 111-312 retroactively patched the AMT for 2010 as well as patching it for 2011. During 2012, there was no AMT patch in place, although ATRA subsequently retroactively applied to 2012.

[26] See Table 1 of CRS Report RL30149, *The Alternative Minimum Tax for Individuals*, by Steven Maguire.

[27] These credits include the adoption tax credit, the dependent care credit, the credit for the elderly and disabled, the child credit, the credit for interest on certain home mortgages, the Hope Scholarship and Lifetime Learning credits, the credit for savers, the credit for certain nonbusiness energy property, the credit for residential energy efficient property, the credit for certain plug-in electric vehicles, the credit for alternative motor vehicles, the credit for new qualified (continued...)

Changes Made by ATRA

ATRA made the AMT patch permanent beginning in 2012. Specifically, ATRA increased the exemption amount to $50,600 for individuals and $78,750 for married couples filing jointly for 2012 and then permanently adjusted these amounts annually for inflation after 2012.[28] It also permanently allowed non-refundable personal credits to be claimed against the AMT.

Budgetary Cost

According to the Joint Committee on Taxation, the permanent extension of the AMT is estimated to reduce revenues by $1.8 trillion over the 10-year budgetary window of 2013-2022 compared to the current law baseline.

Other Expiring Provisions and "Tax Extenders"

Legislative History

In addition to the 2001, 2003, and 2009 tax cuts and the AMT patch, Congress has enacted a variety of other temporary tax provisions that either expired at the end of 2011 or expired at the end of 2012 prior to the enactment of ATRA.[29] These provisions generally fall into one of six categories: those related to individuals, businesses, charitable giving, energy, community development, or disaster relief. **Table 3** provides a list of provisions that expired in 2011 or were scheduled to expire at the end of 2012. In addition, the table includes information as to whether ATRA extended a particular provision. For more information on the historical cost of certain tax extenders (including those not extended by ATRA), see Table 2 in CRS Report R42485, *An Overview of Tax Provisions Expiring in 2012*, by Margot L. Crandall-Hollick.

Importantly, while most of the provisions that expired in 2011 or were scheduled to expire at the end of 2012 have been *routinely* extended on a short-term basis, and are hence commonly referred to as "tax extenders," there are a variety of more recently enacted temporary provisions that have not been previously extended. Both traditional "tax extenders" and these new expiring provisions are included in **Table 3**.

Individual

Several temporary tax provisions affecting individuals either expired at the end of 2011 or were scheduled to expire at the end of 2012. Of these, the largest in terms of estimated revenue losses

---

(...continued)

plug-in electric drive motor vehicles, and the D.C. first-time homebuyer credit.

[28] P.L. 112-240 also adjusts other parameters of the AMT for inflation after 2012, including the tax brackets and the AMT exemption amount phaseout threshold.

[29] Some of temporary tax provisions expire after 2012. A complete list can be found in Joint Committee on Taxation, *List of Expiring Federal Tax Provisions*, January 13, 2012, JCX-1-12. In addition, for an overview of laws which have extended individual provisions, see Table in CRS Report R42105, *Tax Provisions Expiring in 2011 and "Tax Extenders,"* by Molly F. Sherlock.

include the deduction for state and local sales taxes;[30] the above-the-line deduction for qualified tuition and related expenses;[31] the deduction of mortgage insurance premiums as qualified interest; the above-the-line deduction for certain expenses of elementary and secondary school teachers;[32] and the parity in the tax treatment of employer-provided transit benefits to parking benefits.

Business

Several temporary tax provisions affecting businesses either expired at the end of 2011 or were scheduled to expire at the end of 2012. Of these, the largest in terms of estimated revenue losses include bonus depreciation in 2011 and 2012, whereby a 50% bonus depreciation allowance in effect for 2012 was set to expire after December 31, 2012; the research and experimentation credit;[33] the exception under Subpart F for active financing income earned by banking, financing, and insurance business operations abroad;[34] the enhanced cost-recovery for qualified leasehold, restaurant, and retail improvements; and the enhanced expensing allowances which allowed businesses to expense $500,000 in qualified investments in 2011.[35]

Charitable

Several temporary provisions designed to incentivize charitable giving[36] expired at the end of 2011. Of these, the largest in terms of estimated revenue losses was the provision that allowed tax-free distributions from IRAs for the purposes of charitable donations.

Energy

Several temporary provisions affecting the energy sector, including alternative energy, expired at the end of 2011 or were scheduled to expire at the end of 2012. These include incentives for alcohol fuels (primarily ethanol), the Section 1603 grants-in-lieu of tax credit program,[37] incentives for biodiesel and renewable diesel;[38] the placed-in-construction date for the production

---

[30] For more information, see CRS Report RL32781, *Federal Deductibility of State and Local Taxes*, by Steven Maguire.

[31] For more information, see CRS Report R41967, *Higher Education Tax Benefits: Brief Overview and Budgetary Effects*, by Margot L. Crandall-Hollick.

[32] For more information, see CRS Report RS21682, The Tax Deduction for Classroom Expenses of Elementary and Secondary School Teachers, by Linda Levine (out of print; available upon request from author).

[33] For more information, see CRS Report RL31181, *Research Tax Credit: Current Law, Legislation in the 112th Congress, and Policy Issues*, by Gary Guenther.

[34] For more information, see CRS Report R41852, *U.S. International Corporate Taxation: Basic Concepts and Policy Issues*, by Mark P. Keightley.

[35] For more information, see CRS Report RL31852, *Section 179 and Bonus Depreciation Expensing Allowances: Current Law, Legislative Proposals in the 112th Congress, and Economic Effects*, by Gary Guenther.

[36] For more information, see CRS Report RL34608, *Tax Issues Relating to Charitable Contributions and Organizations*, by Jane G. Gravelle and Molly F. Sherlock.

[37] For more information, see CRS Report R41635, *ARRA Section 1603 Grants in Lieu of Tax Credits for Renewable Energy: Overview, Analysis, and Policy Options*, by Phillip Brown and Molly F. Sherlock.

[38] For more information, see CRS Report R40110, *Biofuels Incentives: A Summary of Federal Programs*, by Brent D. Yacobucci.

---

tax credit for wind;[39] and the credit for nonbusiness energy property (sometimes referred to as the "25C credit").[40]

Community Development

Several provisions to promote community development expired at the end of 2011. These include qualified zone academy bonds, which are available to state and local governments for elementary and secondary school renovation, equipment, teacher training, and course materials; the new markets tax credit (NMTC), which is designed to promote investment in low-income and impoverished communities;[41] and tax incentives to encourage economic activity in empowerment zones, and in American Samoa.[42]

Disaster Relief Provisions

A number of disaster-related tax provisions expired at the end of 2011 or were scheduled to expire at the end of 2012. They include provisions designed to help redevelopment of the New York Liberty Zone and the Gulf Opportunity (GO) Zone,[43] as well as provisions to provide relief following the Midwestern storms and Hurricane Ike in 2008.

Changes Made by ATRA

Various temporary expiring provisions and "tax extenders" were extended by ATRA for 2012 (if they expired at the end of 2011) and 2013. For a detailed overview of whether ATRA extended a particular provision, including the budgetary cost of the extension, see **Table 3**. Several temporary expiring provisions, including certain charitable provisions and energy tax provisions (like incentives for alcohol fuel), were not extended by ATRA.

Budgetary Cost

According to the Joint Committee on Taxation, the extension of all temporary expiring provisions and tax extenders through the end of 2013 is estimated to reduce revenues by $76.3 billion over the 10-year budgetary window of 2013-2022. Of these revenue losses, the largest amount of revenue losses is attributable to the extension of provisions for businesses ($46.2 billion). The extension of energy tax extenders is estimated to result in $18.2 billion in revenue losses, while the extension of expiring provisions for individuals is estimated to result in $12.0 billion in revenue losses. The Congressional Budget Office (CBO) has estimated extending *all* expiring provisions *permanently* would reduce revenues by $890 billion over a 10-year budgetary window

---

[39] Prior to H.R. 8, qualifying facilities had to be "placed-in-service" to be eligible for the PTC. P.L. 112-240 modified this requirement so the facility had to be "under construction."

[40] For more information, see CRS Report R42089, *Residential Energy Tax Credits: Overview and Analysis*, by Margot L. Crandall-Hollick and Molly F. Sherlock.

[41] For more information, see CRS Report RL34402, *New Markets Tax Credit: An Introduction*, by Donald J. Marples and Sean Lowry.

[42] For more information, see CRS Report R41639, *Empowerment Zones, Enterprise Communities, and Renewal Communities: Comparative Overview and Analysis*, by Oscar R. Gonzales and Donald J. Marples.

[43] For more information, see CRS Report RS22344, *The Gulf Opportunity Zone Act of 2005*, by Erika K. Lunder.

---

of 2013-2022.[44] For details on the revenue losses over the 10-year budgetary window of 2013-2022 associated with the extension of each provision, see **Table 3**.

---

[44] Congressional Budget Office, *An Update to the Budget and Economic Outlook: Fiscal Years 2012 to 2022*, August 2012, Table 1-5, http://www.cbo.gov/sites/default/files/cbofiles/attachments/08-22-2012-Update_to_Outlook.pdf.

Table 3. Temporary Tax Provisions & "Tax Extenders" Which Expired in 2011 & 2012

Provision	Expired	Internal Revenue Code Section	Extend by ATRA (through Dec. 31, 2013)	10-Year Cost Estimate of ATRA Extension 2013-2022*
Individual Provisions				
Above-the-Line Deduction for Certain Expenses of Elementary and Secondary School Teachers	2011	Sec. 62(a)(2)(D)	YES	$0.4 billion
Deduction for State and Local Sales Taxes	2011	Sec. 164(b)(5)	YES	$5.5 billion
Above-the-Line Deduction for Qualified Tuition and Related Expenses	2011	Sec. 222(e)	YES	$1.7 billion
Estate Tax Look-Through for Certain Regulated Investment Company (RIC) Stock Held by Nonresidents	2011	Sec. 2105(d)	NO	na
Premiums for Mortgage Insurance Deductible as Qualified Interest	2011	Sec. 163(h)(3)	YES	$1.3 billion
Parity for Exclusion for Employer-Provided Mass Transit and Parking Benefits	2011	Sec. 132(f)	YES	$0.2 billion
Disclosure of Prisoner Return Information to Certain Prison Officials	2011	Sec. 6103(k)(10)	YES[a]	$12 million
Treatment of Military Basic Housing Allowance under Low-Income Housing Credit	2011	Sec. 142(d)	YES	$37 million
Expansion of Adoption Credit and Adoption Assistance Programs[b]	2011	Secs. 36C and 137; Sec. 10909(c) of P.L. 111-148	NO	na
Refunds Disregarded in the Administration of Federal Programs and Federally Assisted Programs	2012	Sec. 6409	YES	c
Credit for Prior Year Minimum Tax Liability Made Refundable After Period of Years	2012	Sec. 53(e)	NO	na
Exclusion of Discharge of Principal Residence Indebtedness from Gross Income for Individuals	2012	Sec. 108(a)(1)(E)	YES	$1.3 billion
Business Provisions				
Tax Credit for Research and Experimentation Expenses	2011	Sec. 41(h)(1)(B)	YES	$14.3
Temporary Increase in Limit on Cover-Over of Rum Excise Tax Revenues to Puerto Rico and the Virgin Islands	2011	Sec. 7625(f)	YES	$0.2 billion

Provision	Expired	Internal Revenue Code Section	Extend by ATRA (through Dec. 31, 2013)	10-Year Cost Estimate of ATRA Extension 2013-2022*
Expensing of "Brownfield" Environmental Remediation Costs	2011	Sec. 198(h)	NO	na
Work Opportunity Tax Credit	2011	Sec. 51(c)(4)	YES	$1.8 billion
Indian Employment Tax Credit	2011	Sec. 45A(f)	YES	$0.1 billion
Accelerated Depreciation for Business Property on Indian Reservations	2011	Sec. 168(j)(8)	YES	$0.2 billion
Exceptions under Subpart F for Active Financing Income	2011	Sec. 953(e)(1) and Sec. 954(h)(9)	YES	$11.2 billion
Look-Through Treatment of Payments Between Controlled Foreign Corporations under the Foreign Personal Holding Company Rules	2011	Sec. 954(c)(6)	YES	$1.5 billion
Credit for Railroad Track Maintenance	2011	Sec. 45G(f)	YES	$0.3 billion
15-Year Straight-Line Cost Recovery for Qualified Leasehold, Restaurant, and Retail Improvements	2011	Secs. 168(e)(3)(E)(iv), (v), (ix); Secs.168(e)(7)(A)(i) and 168 (e)(8)	YES	$3.7 billion
7-Year Recovery for Motorsport Racing Facilities	2011	Sec. 168(i)(15) and Sec. 168(e)(3)(C)(ii)	YES	$0.1 billion
Deduction Allowable with Respect to Income Attributable to Domestic Production Activities in Puerto Rico	2011	Sec. 199(d)(8)	YES	$0.4 billion
Modification of Tax Treatment of Certain Payments to Controlling Exempt Organizations	2011	Sec. 512(b)(13)(E)	YES	$40 million
Treatment of Certain Dividends of Regulated Investment Companies ("RICs")	2011	Secs. 871(k)(1)(C) and (2)(C); Secs. 881(e)(1)(A) and (2)	YES	$0.2 billion
Employer Wage Credit for Activated Military Reservists	2011	Sec. 45P	YES	$7 million
Special Expensing Rules for Film and Television Production	2011	Sec. 181(f)	YES	$0.2 billion
RIC Qualified Investment Entity Treatment under FIRPTA	2011	Sec. 897(h)(4)	YES	$60 million

Provision	Expired	Internal Revenue Code Section	Extend by ATRA (through Dec. 31, 2013)	10-Year Cost Estimate of ATRA Extension 2013-2022*
Special Rules for Qualified Small Business Stock	2011	Sec. 1202(a)(4)	YES	$1.0 billion
Additional First-Year Depreciation for 100% of Basis of Qualified Property	2011	Sec. 168(k)(5)	NO	na
Increase in Section 179 Expensing to Amounts/Threshold to $500,000/$2,000,000	2011	Sec. 179(b)(1) and (2) and Sec. 179(f)	YES	$2.4 billion
Reduction in S Corporation Recognition for Built-In Gains Tax	2011	Sec. 1374(d)(7)	YES	$0.3 billion
Work Opportunity Tax Credit Targeted to Hiring Qualified Veterans	2012	Sec. 51(c)(4)(B)	YES	$0.1 billion
Additional First-Year Depreciation for 50 Percent of Basis of Qualified Property	2012	Sec. 168(k)(1) and Sec. 168(k)(2)	YES	$4.7 billion
Election to Accelerate AMT Credits in Lieu of Additional First-Year Depreciation	2012	Sec. 168(k)(4)	YES	$0.3 billion
Charitable Provisions				
Enhanced Charitable Deduction for Corporate Contributions of Computer Equipment for Educational Purposes	2011	Sec. 170(e)(6)	NO	na
Enhanced Charitable Deduction for Contributions of Food Inventory	2011	Sec. 170(e)(3)(C)	YES	$0.3 billion
Enhanced Charitable Deduction for Contributions of Book Inventory to Public Schools	2011	Sec. 170(e)(3)(D)	NO	na
Tax-Free Distributions from Individual Retirement Accounts for Charitable Purposes	2011	Sec. 408(d)(8)	YES	$1.3 billion
Basis Adjustment to Stock of S Corporations Making Charitable Contributions of Property	2011	Sec. 1367(a)	YES	$0.2 billion
Special Rules for Contributions of Capital Gain Real Property for Conservation Purposes	2011	Sec. 170(b)(1)(E) and Sec. 170(b)(2)(B)	YES	$0.3 billion
Energy Provisions				
Suspensions of 100%-of-Net-Income Limitation on Percentage Depletion for Oil and Gas from Marginal Wells	2011	Sec. 613A(c)(6)(H)(ii)	NO	na
Special Rule to Implement FERC or Electric Transmission Restructuring	2011	Sec. 451(i)	YES	—
Credit for Construction of Energy Efficient New Homes	2011	Sec. 45L(g)	YES	$0.2 billion

An Overview of the Tax Provisions in the American Taxpayer Relief Act of 2012

Provision	Expired	Internal Revenue Code Section	Extend by ATRA (through Dec. 31, 2013)	10-Year Cost Estimate of ATRA Extension 2013-2022*
Placed-in-Service Date for Refined Coal Production Facilities	2011	Sec.45(d)(8)	NO	na
Mine Rescue Team Training Credit	2011	Sec. 45N	YES	$5 million
Election to Expense Mine-Safety Equipment	2011	Sec. 179E(a)	YES	—
Credit for Energy Efficient Appliances	2011	Sec. 45M(b)	YES	$0.7 billion
Credit for Nonbusiness Energy Property	2011	Sec. 25C(g)	YES	$2.5 billion
Alternative Fuel Vehicle Refueling Property	2011	Sec. 30C(g)(2)	YES	$44 million
Incentives for Alternative Fuel and Alternative Fuel Mixtures	2011	Sec. 6426(d)(5). Sec.6427(e)(6)(C), Sec. 6426(e)(3)	YES	$0.4 billion
Incentives for Biodiesel and Renewable Diesel	2011	Sec. 40A; Sec, 6426(c)(6); and Sec. 6427(e)(6)(B)	YES	$2.2 billion
Incentives for Alcohol Fuels	2011	Sec. 40(e)(1)(A); Secs.40(h)(1) and (h)(2); Sec.6426(b)(6); Sec. 6427(e)(6)(A)	NO	na
Grants for Specified Energy Property in Lieu of Tax Credits	2011	Sec. 48(d) and Sec. 1603 of P.L. 111-5	NO	na
Credit for Electric Drive Motorcycles, Three-Wheeled, and Low-Speed Vehicles	2011	Sec. 30(f)	YES	$7 million
Conversion Credit for Plug-In Electric Vehicles	2011	Sec. 30B(i)(4)	NO	na
Qualified Green Building and Sustainable Design Project Bonds	2012	Sec. 142(l)(9)	NO	na
Cellulosic Biofuel Producer Credit	2012	Sec. 40(b)(6)(H)	YES	$59 million[d]
Construction Date for Eligible Facilities (Including Wind) to Claim the Electricity Production Credit	2012	Sec. 45(d)	YES	$12.2 billion[e]
Credit for Production of Indian Coal	2012	Sec. 45(e)(10)(A)(i)	YES	$1 million

An Overview of the Tax Provisions in the American Taxpayer Relief Act of 2012

Provision	Expired	Internal Revenue Code Section	Extend by ATRA (through Dec. 31, 2013)	10-Year Cost Estimate of ATRA Extension 2013-2022*
Election to Claim the Energy Credit in Lieu of the Electricity Production Credit	2012	Sec.48(a)(5)	YES	$0.1 billion
Special Depreciation Allowance for Cellulosic Biofuel Plant Property^f	2012	Sec. 168(l)	YES	$500,000
Community Development Provisions				
Qualified Zone Academy Bonds – Allocation of Bond Limitation	2011	Sec. 54E(c)(1)	YES	$0.2 billion
New Markets Tax Credit	2011	Sec. 45D(f)(1)	YES	$1.8 billion
American Samoa Economic Development Credit	2011	Sec. 119 of P.L. 109-432 as amended by Sec.756 of P.L. 111-312	YES	$62 million
Tax Incentives for Investment in the District of Columbia ("DC")	2011	Sec. 1400(f)(1), Sec. 1400A(b), Sec. 1400B(b)(2)(A)(i), Sec. 1400B(b)(3)(A), Sec. 1400B(b)(4)(A)(i). Sec.1400B(b)(4)(B)(i)(I), Sec. 1400B(e)(2) and Sec. 1400B(g)(2)	NO	na
Empowerment Zone Tax Incentives	2011	Sec. 1391(d)(1)(A)(i), Sec. 1391(h)(2), Sec. 1202(a)(2), Sec. 1394, Sec. 1396, Sec. 1397A, Sec. 1397B	YES	$0.5 billion
Disaster Relief Provisions				
New York Liberty Zone – Tax Exempt Bond Financing	2011	Sec. 1400L(d)(2)(D)	YES	g
Tax-Exempt Bond Financing for the Gulf Opportunity (GO) Zone	2011	Sec. 1400N(a)	NO	na
Low-Income Housing Credit Additional Credit for the GO Zone	2011	Sec. 1400N(c)	NO	na
Placed-in-Service Date for Additional Depreciation for specified GO Zone Extension Property	2011	Sec, 1400N(d)(6)	NO	na

An Overview of the Tax Provisions in the American Taxpayer Relief Act of 2012

Provision	Expired	Internal Revenue Code Section	Extend by ATRA (through Dec. 31, 2013)	10-Year Cost Estimate of ATRA Extension 2013-2022*
Increase in Rehabilitation Credit for Structures Located in the GO Zone	2011	Sec. 1400N(h)	NO	na
Increase in Rehabilitation Credit for Areas Damaged by the 2008 Midwestern Storms	2011	Sec. 702 of Division C of P.L. 110-343	NO	na
Tax-Exempt Bond Financing for Areas Damaged by the 2008 Midwestern Storms	2012	Sec. 702 of Division C of P.L. 110-343	NO	na
Tax-Exempt Bond Financing for Areas Damaged by Hurricane Ike in 2008	2012	Sec. 704 of Division C of P.L. 110-343	NO	na

Source: Joint Committee on Taxation, *List of Expiring Federal Tax Provisions*, January 13, 2012, JCX-1-1, Joint Committee on Taxation, *Estimated Revenue Effects of the Revenue Provisions Contained in an Amendment in the Nature of a Substitute to H.R. 8, the "American Taxpayer Relief Act of 2012" as Passed by the Senate on January 1, 2013*, January 1, 2013. JCX-1-13 and Table 2 in CRS Report R42485, *An Overview of Tax Provisions Expiring in 2012*, by Margot L. Crandall-Hollick.

Notes: * Revenue changes associated with the short-term extension of certain provisions may occur in years after the provision has expired. In order to allow a comparison of the costs of these tax provisions, the revenue losses which occur over a 10-year budgetary window are provided. For revenue losses for each fiscal year, see JCX-1-13. In addition to the provisions included in this table, ATRA also created a low income housing credit floor of 9 percent. JCT estimates this will reduce revenues by $8 million over the 10-year budgetary window of 2013-2022. ATRA also extended the housing allowance exclusions for determining median gross income for qualified residential rental project exempt facilities.

"na" = a revenue loss estimate of extending the provision is unavailable because the provision was not extended as part of P.L. 112-240.

"____" = no revenue loss.

a.   This provisions was permanently extended.

b.   For more information, see CRS Report RL33633, *Tax Benefits for Families: Adoption*, by Christine Scott.

c.   Estimates of S. 3521 indicate that the extension of this provision for one year (2013) would result in less than $10 million of revenue losses over a 10-year period (2013-2022). A revenue loss estimate for the permanent extension of this provision as included in P.L. 112-240 is not available.

d.   The maximum credit would be $1.01 per gallon and would apply to fuel from algae.

e.   The placed in service date for the PTC for wind was scheduled to expire at the end of 2012, while the placed in service date for the PTC for other renewable technologies were generally scheduled to expire at the end of 2013. Prior to ATRA, extensions of the PTC extended the placed-in-service date for eligible properties. Hence if a wind facility was operating prior to the expiration date, they would be eligible for the credit. The extension of the PTC for wind included a provision that modified the expiration date for all renewable technologies (including wind) such that qualified facilities will be eligible for the PTC (or the investment tax credit in lieu of the production tax credit) if the construction—as opposed to the placed in service date—begins prior to the end of 2013. In addition, the renewable energy production tax credit was also modified to exclude segregate paper from the definition of municipal solid water eligible for the credit.

f. Algae is considered a qualified feedstock for this tax provisions.

g. JCT estimates the extension of this provision has no revenue effect.

In-Plan Roth Conversions

Legislative History

Many employers offer their employees tax-deferred retirement plans. Specifically, employees may elect to contribute a portion of their *pre-tax* compensation (i.e., tax-deductible) to a retirement plan, such as a 401(k). These contributions are not taxed when the funds are contributed to the plan or as earnings accrue; rather they are taxed when the employee withdraws these funds from the retirement account. At that point, the withdrawn funds (referred to as "distributions") are included as taxable income and taxed at ordinary income tax rates (not capital gains rates).

More recently, some employers have begun to offer their employees "Roth contribution programs," sometimes called "Roth 401(k)s" (employers may also maintain Roth 403(b) and Roth 457 plans). Unlike other employer-sponsored plans, these programs allow employees to elect to contribute some of their *post-tax* compensation (i.e., not tax-deductible) to an account called a Roth contribution account.[45] Since these contributions are taxed when the funds are contributed to the Roth plan, they are generally[46] not taxed when the employee withdraws these funds from the plan.

At the end of 2010, Congress enacted the Small Business Jobs Act (P.L. 111-240), which permitted in-plan Roth rollovers from retirement plan funds (i.e., money in traditional 401(k), 403(b), and 457 plans) *that were eligible for distribution* to a designated Roth contribution program in the same plan, like a "Roth 401(k)."[47] Importantly, according to this 2010 law, funds eligible for the "in-Plan Roth rollover" had to be otherwise eligible to be withdrawn or "distributable" under the retirement plan. Generally, "distributable" funds from a retirement plan refer to the employees' vested balance once they reach 59 ½ years of age or the designated retirement age for that plan.[48] In other words, as a result of the changes included in P.L. 111-240, employees who had reached 59 ½ years old could elect to roll over their vested balance from their 401(k) plan to a Roth 401(k), but other employees would not necessarily be eligible for these conversions.[49] When the rollover occurred, the funds which were rolled over—and were not

---

[45] Unlike a Roth-IRA account, which can be established by any individual who works, a Roth 401(k), Roth 403(b), and Roth 457 accounts are established by an employer who maintains a traditional 401(k), 403(b), 457 account. In addition, while Roth-IRAs are available only to taxpayers with adjusted gross incomes below a certain level, Roth contribution programs are available to any employee, regardless of income level, who is a participant in a 401(k) or 403(b) plan that allows Roth deferrals. For more information on Roth IRAs, see CRS Report RL34397, *Traditional and Roth Individual Retirement Accounts (IRAs): A Primer*, by John J. Topoleski.

[46] In order for a withdrawal to qualify for tax-free status, it must fulfill two requirements: it must be made after the five-taxable year period beginning with the first taxable year for which the individual made a contribution to a Roth IRA and (2) it must be made after the beneficiary reaches 59 ½, or is made on account of death or disability or is made for first-time homebuyer expenses of up to $10,000.

[47] IRC § 402A(c)(4). For more information, see IRS Notice 2010-84, at http://www.irs.gov/irb/2010-51_IRB/ar11.html; Joint Committee on Taxation, *Technical Explanation of the Tax provisions in Senate Amendment 4594 to H.R. 5297, the "Small Business Jobs Act of 2010," Scheduled for Consideration by the Senate on September 16, 2010.* September 16, 2010, JCX-47-10, p. 42.

[48] See, for example, IRS Notice 2010-84 at http://www.irs.gov/irb/2010-51_IRB/ar11.html; Rev. Rul. 2004-12, 2004-1 C.B. 478 at http://www.irs.gov/irb/2004-07_IRB/ar08.html.

[49] A retirement plan would have to allow contributors to designate contributions as Roth contributions.

---

previously subject to tax—would be subject to income tax, generating revenue at the time of the conversion. However, when the funds were ultimately withdrawn from the Roth contribution program, they would no longer be subject to tax. Tax revenue is thus collected earlier than if the conversion were not allowed.

Changes Made by ATRA

P.L. 112-240 expanded the changes made by P.L. 111-240 to allow virtually all traditional 401(k), 403(b), and 457 plan account balances to be transferred to Roth Contribution programs,[50] effectively removing the requirement that funds from these accounts be otherwise "distributable."[51,52] As discussed, prior to ATRA only funds from retirement accounts that could be withdrawn—generally the vested balance once the employee had reached retirement age—could be converted into a Roth contribution plan. The change included in Title X of P.L. 112-240 raises revenue over the next 10 years by collecting taxes on the money converted from traditional 401(k) (or 403(b) or 457 plan) accounts to Roth 401(k) (or 403(b) or 457) plans.

When an employee ultimately withdraws the funds from a Roth contribution plan, the distribution will be tax-free. Hence, by electing to convert a non-Roth account to a Roth account, an employee will pay tax at the time the funds are rolled over or converted, which will raise revenues for the federal government at the time the roll-over or conversion occurs. If the funds were not converted, but remained in the tax-deferred retirement account, taxes would be collected in later years when the funds were actually withdrawn. Hence, this provision effectively shifts the timing of tax payments, raising more revenue in the short run and less revenue in the long run.

Budgetary Cost

Title X of P.L. 112-240 *raises* $12.2 billion in revenue over the 10-year budgetary window of FY2013-FY2022 (revenue losses occur outside the budget window). These funds were characterized as partially offsetting a $24 billion reduction in automatic spending cuts (sequester) scheduled to occur in FY2013. For more information about the sequester and P.L. 112-240, see CRS Report R42884, *The "Fiscal Cliff" and the American Taxpayer Relief Act of 2012*, coordinated by Mindy R. Levit.

Author Contact Information

Margot L. Crandall-Hollick
Analyst in Public Finance
mcrandallhollick@crs.loc.gov, 7-7582

---

[50] This provision also is applicable to conversion of funds in the Thrift Savings Plan (TSP) to a Roth –TSP.

[51] According to recent reports, this may greatly increase the amount of money in traditional employer-sponsored retirement plans that can be converted into Roth plans. See Ashlea Ebeling, "Roth 401(k) Conversions for All Thanks To Fiscal Cliff Deal," *Forbes*, January 2, 2013

[52] For both the TSP and the other retirement accounts, this provision allows them to offer participants the option to convert; it does not require the plan to have the option.